Chasing a serial killer

BE A CRIMINAL PROFILER

by Alix Wood

Gareth Stevens
PUBLISHING

Please visit our website, **www.garethstevens.com**. For a free color catalog of all our high-quality books, call toll free 1-800-542-2595 or fax 1-877-542-2596

Cataloging-in-Publication Data
Names: Wood, Alix.
Title: Chasing a serial killer: be a criminal profiler / Alix Wood.
Description: New York : Gareth Stevens Publishing, 2018. | Series: Crime solvers | Includes index.
Identifiers: ISBN 9781538206362 (pbk.) | ISBN 9781538206300 (library bound) |
   ISBN 9781538206188 (6 pack)
Subjects: LCSH: Criminal behavior, Prediction of--Juvenile literature. | Criminal profilers--
   Juvenile literature. | Criminal investigation--Juvenile literature.
Classification: LCC HV6027.W66 2018 | DDC 363.25'8--dc23

First Edition

Published in 2018 by
Gareth Stevens Publishing
111 East 14th Street, Suite 349
New York, NY 10003

Copyright © 2018 Alix Wood Books

Produced for Gareth Stevens by Alix Wood Books
Designed by Alix Wood
Editor: Eloise Macgregor
Consultant: Stacey Deville, MFS, Texas Forensic Investigative
Consultants

Photo credits:
Cover, 1, 4-5, 6, 7, 8, 9, 10, 12, 15, 16, 18, 19, 20, 21, 22, 24, 25, 27 bottom, 28, 29, 30 , 34, 35, 36, 37, 38, 39, 41, 42, 43 © Adobe Stock Images, 27 top, 31, 32 © Alix Wood, 33 © Henry T. Phillips, all other images are in the public domain

Printed in the United States of America
CPSIA compliance information: Batch #CS17GS For further information contact Gareth Stevens, New York, New York at 1-800-542-2595.

CONTENTS

call a criminal profiler...

Detectives are called to an apartment in downtown Saunderstone. A man has been found dead. Detectives can't see an obvious cause of death. They send the body for an **autopsy**. An autopsy is a detailed examination to find out what caused someone to die.

Forensic pathologist Prisha Gupta sets to work examining the body. The victim is a young man. He seems perfectly healthy, apart from the fact that he is dead! This is the third strange case like this that Prisha has seen in the last six months. The other two turned out to have been poisoned...

DISPATCHER: Emergency 911. What is the location of your emergency?

PATTY: I'm at 1417, Belleview Apartments in Saunderstone.

DISPATCHER: What is your emergency, caller?

PATTY: It's my husband. Help. I think he is dead. He's not breathing...

Pathologist's Report

Autopsy performed on: Jonathan Garcia
Age: 29
Profession: Computer programmer

Findings: An otherwise healthy man. No signs of recent injury. No sign of any existing illness.

Stomach contents: A last meal of what appeared to be a type of game, possibly quail, potatoes, and salad. Samples of the stomach contents have been sent to the laboratory for tests, to check if they contained poison.

Cause of Death: Breathing failure, probably caused by poisoning.

Autopsy

Detective Doug Smithson comes to talk to Prisha. He's also concerned that this death is similar to two other recent poisoning cases. Prisha agrees. Once the lab team tests this victim's stomach contents, they will know for sure if he was killed with the same poison. It looks like Saunderstone may have a **serial killer** on the loose. This case may need the services of a criminal profiler.

Solve It!

Can you guess how many separate murders makes someone a "serial killer"?

a) two

b) three

c) four

Answers on page 45

meet a criminal profiler

Criminal profiler Tobias Johnson is busy in his office finishing up his report on his last case. A call comes through from Detective Doug Smithson. He wants Tobias to look at his recent poisoning cases. The victims seem to have nothing in common except the poison they died from. Even though the lab results haven't come back from the latest case, Doug wants to start putting a profile together. If there is a serial killer in Saunderstone, Doug wants to catch them before they kill again.

Criminal profilers use their skills to identify the type of person who most likely committed a crime. Tobias bases his profiles on his knowledge of the type of person who usually commits that type of crime.

Name: **Tobias Johnson**

Job: Criminal Profiler

Education: Studied for a degree in Criminal Justice, then studied for a Master's in Psychology

Previous jobs: Police Officer

Career: Tobias worked for the police force for three years after getting his Master's degree.

Favorite school subjects: History and Biology.

Favorite part of his job: Working with all kinds of different people.

Worst part of his job: Paperwork!

Most interesting case: Tobias once worked on a series of murders of university professors. There were no witnesses, and the murderer left no **DNA** or fingerprint **evidence**. Police needed something to go on. After studying the **crime scenes**, Tobias drew up a profile of the killer. He believed that the killer had a university education, but was now a loner, living in or near the university. The murderer was probably male, white, unemployed or working a low-paid job, and living on his own. Police put out an appeal for the public to think who might match the description. The murderer was caught after a man became suspicious of his neighbor.

Personnel File

Inking the Crimes

Doug comes to see Tobias at his office and shows him the case files. The first poisoning death had not seemed suspicious at first. Jillie Hazel was found dead in her bed one morning by her roommate. Jillie had died of a breathing failure. As she suffered from asthma, the detectives and her family and friends thought that her illness must have caused her death. It was only after the autopsy that detectives released she was probably poisoned. Traces of the deadly poison hemlock plant were found in her stomach.

Top Tip

The hemlock plant is poisonous. It often grows by the roadside, near rivers, and on open land. People can mistake it for wild carrots or parsley — with deadly results!

A second poisoning victim was discovered two months later. Summer Jones got sick while walking her dog. Summer was a healthy fitness enthusiast, so everyone was baffled when she suddenly died. Her autopsy also showed traces of poisonous hemlock. Nothing about the two victims seemed to link them together. Police were struggling to find a connection that might lead them to the killer.

EVIDENCE BAG CHALLENGE

Can you find any links between the Hemlock Poisoner's first two victims, Jillie Hazel and Summer Jones?

Victim One

Jillie Hazel
Apartment 26,
324 Valley View,
Saunderstone
Age: 22
Occupation: student
Marital Status: single
Cause of death: breathing
    failure
Found by: her roommate
    Alice Pomfrett
Ambulance called by:
    passerby
Last meal: fried chicken,
    fries, corn

Victim Two

Summer Jones
1206 Maple Street,
Saunderstone
Age: 37
Occupation: personal
    trainer
Marital Status: married
Cause of death: breathing
    failure
Found by: a park ice cream
    seller
Ambulance called by:
    passerby
Last meal: fresh salad,
    tuna, couscous

Answers on page 45

Put Yourself in Their Shoes

When detectives hunt criminals, it helps to try to understand how the criminals' minds work. This helps detectives guess their next move. Criminal profilers have usually studied for a Bachelor's or Master's degree in Psychology.

Solve It!

What is Psychology?

a) the study of how the human body works

b) the study of how human minds work and influence how we behave

Answers on page 45

Top Tip

Profilers try to imagine what life is like seen through the eyes of the person they are hunting.

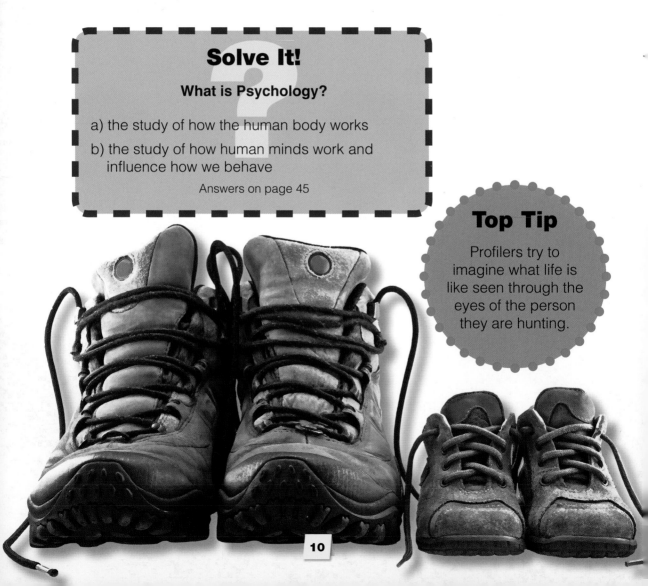

Have you ever tried to "put yourself in someone else's shoes"? It can be a really great way to understand other people. Try to imagine what it would be like to be the people in these typical school situations. Imagining how they feel also might help you guess what they may do next.

1. Your friend falls over in front of everyone.

2. You helped your friend find the right classroom.

3. Your friend's dog is very ill.

4. Your friend gets a bad grade.

5. Your friend has to speak in front of the whole class.

6. Your friend is being teased by a bully.

a DISAPPOINTED

b SAD

c EMBARRASSED

d NERVOUS

e GRATEFUL

f WORRIED

It's not very nice to try to imagine what someone as unpleasant as a serial killer is thinking! Criminal profilers have to put themselves in this position, though. They have to be the kinds of people who don't let the bad things they see affect them too much.

CLOSE LOOK

Jonathan Garcia
Apartment 14,
673 Parkside,
Saunderstone
Age: 29
Occupation: computer
programmer
Marital Status: married
Cause of death: breathing
failure
Found by: his wife,
Patty Garcia
Ambulance called by:
his wife
Last meal: quail, potatoes,
salad

The results are back from the lab! The latest victim, Jonathan Garcia, had traces of hemlock in his system. A serial killer is definitely on the loose in Saunderstone. The investigating team meets to discuss what they know, and what they should do next.

Tobias is asked to draw up a criminal profile. The first thing Tobias needs to do is to study the crimes themselves. Tobias reads through the police and autopsy reports. He can find information for his profiles in even the smallest details.

CRIME SCENE DO NOT CROSS

Analyzing the Crime Scenes

Is there any connection with where the victims died?	Two died at home, one outside, so probably not.
Was the poisoner present when they died?	Probably not, but may have been waiting nearby.
How did the killer poison them?	Most likely in food they ate.
Did the killer know the victims?	Likely, as they probably poisoned the victims' food.
Could the person who found the victims be the killer?	Unlikely, they were found by a friend, a partner, and a stranger.
Does anything link the victims?	They are all young and healthy.
How long did it take for the poison to kill them?	The poison was eaten several hours before death.

Top Tip

When putting together a profile, it is best for the profiler not to know anything about possible **suspects**. This may accidentally influence the profiler and cause them to make a profile match a suspect.

Solve It!

A criminal profile describes a type of person rather than an actual person. Which of these descriptions would most likely be used when making a criminal profile?

a) the killer probably had few friends

b) the killer could be Patty Garcia

c) The killer might be the park's ice cream seller

Answers on page 45

Organized or Disorganized?

A profiler can usually tell if a killer is organized or disorganized by examining the crime scene. A crime scene will usually have plenty of clues. Finding this information out is very useful. Organized criminals have a very different criminal profile from disorganized ones.

Top Tip

Some criminals are classified as "mixed," because they show a mixture of organized and disorganized behavior.

A Typical Crime Scene

Organized

The crime shows evidence of being planned ahead.

The criminal would have brought any tools they needed with them.

An organized murderer would generally hide the body.

They will usually wipe away any evidence, such as fingerprints, so as not to get caught.

Disorganized

The disorganized criminal would have used tools and murder weapons found at the scene. They would not have brought anything with them.

The crime scene is messy.

They would have left the body at the crime scene.

They often leave evidence, such as fingerprints, at the crime scene.

EVIDENCE BAG CHALLENGE

Can you tell the difference between an organized crime scene and a disorganized crime scene? Try this experiment yourself. You are going to perform this experiment two times. The first time mimics what a disorganized criminal might act like, the second time mimics an organized criminal. Do you think you could tell which was which by just looking at the scene?

You will need: two large trays full of soil or sand, ten small coins, a timer, a friend, an old comb

1. Ask a friend to hide the ten coins in the sand tray, and then comb the sand. Look away so you don't see where they put them. Set the timer to ten seconds. Find as many coins as you can in the time.

2. Your friend now hides all ten coins in the second tray while you are watching. Repeat the experiment. This time should be easier. You should get time to tidy the sand with the comb at the end.

3. Look at both trays. Is there a difference between the two "crime scenes"?

reating a Profile

Once Tobias knows which kind of criminal he is dealing with he can start working out their profile. He bases his profile on his own experience and years of research by other profilers.

Organized criminals tend to be more intelligent. They usually have a job and a partner. They usually target a particular type of victim. Disorganized offenders tend to live alone or with a relative. They usually have lower than average intelligence. Disorganized criminals often do not have a job, or have a low-paid job.

Solve It!

What type of serial killer do you think the Hemlock Poisoner might be?

a) organized

b) disorganized

Answers on page 45

Organizations such as the FBI (Federal Bureau of Investigation) log crimes into a database. Over time, profilers can see similarities in the way crimes were committed and the types of criminals who committed them. This information helps them be sure their profiles are based on facts, and not just hunches.

EVIDENCE BAG CHALLENGE

How many crimes do you think you would have to study to be sure that similarities aren't just **coincidence**? Sample size is very important. The more people you study, the more likely it is that your results are correct. See if you can prove this by trying this experiment. Test whether drinking an energy drink helps people react quicker.

You will need: an energy drink, ten friends, a table, a ruler

1 Choose two friends. Give one an energy drink. Have each friend in turn stand with their hand out in front of them. Hold a ruler just above their open hand. When you release the ruler they must grab it as fast as they can.

2 Record where on the ruler each friend caught it. Whose reaction was quickest? Does that prove anything?

3 Now try it with all ten friends, with half of them drinking the energy drink. Did your results change? Which results are more accurate, do you think — the results after testing two people, or after testing ten people?

Why Them?

The type of victim a criminal chooses can give investigators a lot of clues about the killer. It can also help them predict whom the killer might target next. Tobias studies all the victims to help him build a profile.

Top Tip

Victims are usually **vulnerable** in some way. They are often very old, very young, weak, or unaware of the danger signs around them.

Solve It!

Serial killers don't usually target young, strong, healthy victims. Why?

a) because young victims don't have much money

b) because they might be stronger than the serial killer and get away

c) because they like healthy people

Answers on page 45

Is the Hemlock Poisoner killing people at random, or choosing their victims carefully? Do the victims have anything in common? Tobias has already noticed the three victims are all unusually young and healthy. Could that be the type of victim the killer wants to target?

Poisoners can be far from their victims when they die. It doesn't matter if the victims are bigger or stronger than the poisoner. Usually, though, serial killers behave more like a wild animal hunting their prey. They will go for the lone, weaker animals that are easiest to catch.

EVIDENCE BAG CHALLENGE

There are some fun outdoor games that give you an idea what it is like to be an animal hunting prey. Try playing Hunter and Guard with some friends.

You will need: some friends, an outdoor area, a stick or chalk

1. Choose one player to be the hunter. Another player is the guard. The rest become animals.

2. Using a stick or chalk, mark out a circle in the middle of the playing area. This "pen" needs to be big enough for all the players to stand in, once they've been caught. The guard stands in the pen and guards it.

3. The animals run around the play area. If the hunter catches an animal, they are taken to the pen. Captured animals can be rescued on the way to the pen by one of the other animals touching them. The rescuer mustn't be touched by the hunter or the guard, or they will be put in the pen, too.

A Fact or an Assumption?

Some people think that criminal profilers do not really help investigations. They believe they just create **stereotypes**. A stereotype is a general idea people have about a person that is often untrue or only partly true. Saying something like "all people who wear glasses are clever" is a stereotype. How well your eyes work has nothing to do with how well your brain works. But of course, plenty of people who wear glasses are clever.

Criminal profiles can seem like stereotypes. Profilers have to make assumptions about the type of person who committed the crime. They make their assumption after studying the facts of many other cases, though. They try hard not to be **prejudiced**.

Top Tip

Which of these two boys is the smartest? Answer — you can't tell just by looking at them!

Are You Prejudiced?

Do you think that you judge people just on the way they look? Cover the upside-down photographs at the bottom of the page. Then study the faces in the photographs below. Match each person with the job that you think they do. Uncover the photos at the bottom of the page. Were you right? Try the test on some friends.

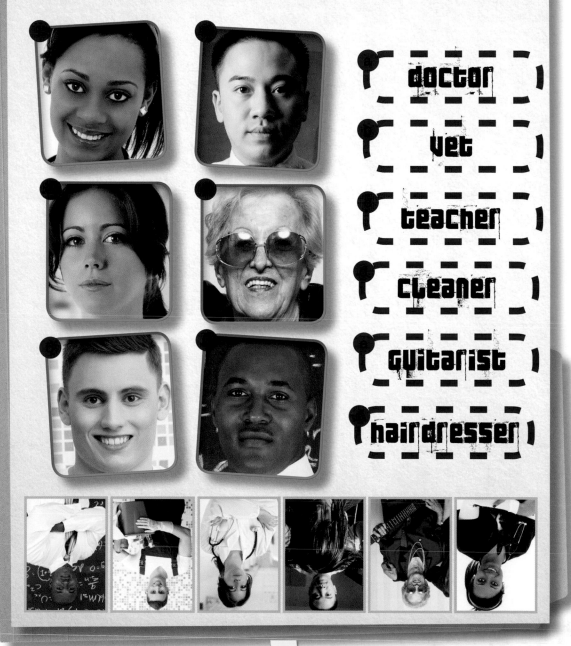

doctor

vet

teacher

cleaner

guitarist

hairdresser

Risk Taker?

How much of a risk taker do you think the Hemlock Poisoner is? A crime scene usually gives Tobias plenty of information about how much risk a criminal is prepared to take. For instance, crimes done in broad daylight usually run more risk of being seen than crimes done after dark.

Tobias does not think that the Hemlock Poisoner is a risk taker. Poisoners usually aren't. The poison might be eaten or drunk without the killer even being present. They can be a long way from their victim when the poison starts to work. There is often no obvious crime scene.

Solve It!

Which of these crimes would most likely be done by a risk taker?

a) a burglary on a city street in the very early hours of the morning

b) a burglary at a lonely farmhouse in the middle of the day

c) a burglary on a busy street in the middle of the day

Answers on page 45

EVIDENCE BAG CHALLENGE

Are you a risk taker? Look at the examples below and decide which way you would choose.

1 You are captaining your football team. In the last seconds of the game you have the choice between calling two plays. One play would mean almost certainly scoring 3 points to tie the game. The other riskier play might result in a touchdown, meaning you would win the game if you succeeded, but lose if you failed. Which do you choose?

a [risk it]   **b** [don't risk it]

2 You work a paper route. You earn $3 a day. You had to wait a few months to get the job and there are kids waiting to take over from you if you leave. A friend has offered you $4 a day helping him sell lemonade. He has only just started selling it, and doesn't know how long the job might last. What do you do?

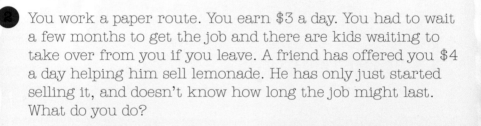

a [risk it]   **b** [don't risk it]

People take risks for a variety of reasons. They might not believe that they will get caught. Some people may feel forced into taking a risk — perhaps they were surprised and had to act suddenly. Other risk takers actually like the excitement of the risk itself. Some people don't really care if they get caught, or may actually want to get caught.

Why Did They Kill?

Getting into the mind of a serial killer is a pretty unpleasant thing to do. Luckily, not many people think like they do!

Understanding the killer's **motive** will help Tobias understand what kind of person they are. This will help to catch them before they hurt anyone else. A motive is the reason behind why someone does something. Most serial killers have had a difficult childhood, and they may have some form of **mental illness**, too. These issues can affect a serial killer's motive.

Killer Motives

Serial killers can be motivated in a number of ways:

- Anger - they might dislike certain types of people

- Power - they might enjoy feeling powerful over their victims

- Money - they might gain money by killing, particularly if they might **inherit** money after family members' deaths

Tobias can't be sure of the Hemlock Poisoner's motive yet. He is more likely to find a possible reason once he can see a connection between the victims, or between the victims and the killer.

He checks out the victims' families to see if there is anyone who knows all the victims. He finds no one. This case is puzzling.

Top Tip

Sometimes, the criminal is the only one who ever knows the motive behind a crime.

SCIENCE DETECTIVE

Working Out the M.O.

M.O. stands for "modus operandi." A modus operandi is a particular method a criminal uses to commit a crime. For example, they might always use the same tools to break into a house. A profiler may use a criminal's M.O. to help build up a picture of what kind of person the criminal is.

Can you match the questions Tobias may ask himself about an M.O. to the **conclusions** he may be able to make?

1

Question:
What type of transportation did they use?

a

Conclusion:
Are they a loner? Or do they have a trusted friend?

2

Question:
Did the criminal strike during the day or night?

b

Conclusion:
Could the skills point to a job they have, or have had in the past?

3

Question:
Did they possess any particular skills to commit their crime?

c

Conclusion:
They must have access to a vehicle.

4

Question:
Did they commit the crime alone or with someone else?

d

Conclusion:
Their job may mean they are only able to commit crimes at a certain time of day.

EVIDENCE BAG CHALLENGE

Set up this M.O. challenge. See if your friends would all tackle this problem in a different way.

You will need: three or four friends, some thick gloves, a small box, wrapping paper and tape, a plastic knife, fork, and spoon

1. Wrap the box in two layers of wrapping paper. Ask each friend to put on the gloves and then try to unwrap the box. They must only use the knife, fork, or spoon.

2. Wrap up the box again and get the next friend to try.

3. Record what "tool" each friend uses. Does each friend have a different M.O.? Which friend unwraps the box the easiest?

Sometimes serial killers take a souvenir from their victim, such as a piece of jewelry. This can be a big mistake. If such a souvenir is found at the killer's home, this helps police provide evidence that they committed the murder.

This poisoner's M.O. is providing the victim with food laced with hemlock. Detectives have been trying to find out where the poisoned food came from. The victims had all eaten different types of food. However, all the victims had recently been to a health food store on Third Street. Detective Smithson went to the store to interview the staff, and find out who supplied the shop with food and medicine. He took Tobias's profile notes with him.

Criminal Profile Notes

Organized. Intelligent. Probably has a job and a partner. Could be a woman. Could be someone who is weaker than the victims. Not a risk taker. Has knowledge of plants or chemistry. Has access to food and drugs in the store.

Sarah Crowther works at the checkout. She lives with her parents. She is studying chemistry part-time. She wants to be a pharmacist. She doesn't prepare any of the food or medicines.

Ahmed Ishak is the butcher who supplies the store with meat. He lives with his partner. He likes skydiving and walking in the countryside.

Pharmacist **José Marquez** lives alone. He prepares the drugs in the store but has no contact with any of the food. He is a vegetarian and does not like to touch meat.

Store owner **Patricia Nilsson** has run the store since leaving her job managing a garden center. She is married to a poultry farmer. She likes reading. She helps out in every department of the store if staff are off sick.

Solve It!

Who do you think best fits Tobias's criminal profile up to now?

a) Sarah Crowther

b) Ahmed Ishak

c) José Marquez

d) Patricia Nilsson

Answers on page 45

Recreating the Scene

Sometimes a profiler will write a **reconstruction** to help understand what happened at a crime scene. They will piece together the evidence and try to work out how the crime played out. Profilers need to be very good at **critical thinking**. To think critically about a problem means to be open-minded and consider all the different possible solutions.

From the evidence you can see, what do you think happened here? There are no blood stains, so why are there four bullet casings? Did the killer drop them or place them? Was the death an accident? Was the victim hit by the log, or the lamp, or the chair? Or did they use them to defend themselves? Profilers must base their reconstruction on hard evidence, not guesses. There is not much hard evidence here.

Some crime scenes have evidence that can be used to build a profile. Footprints may come into the scene from a certain direction. Maybe they were made by a specific type of boot. Who would come from that direction, and wear that boot? A rear window had been forced open. Did the killer know the back of the building well enough to choose that entry point?

EVIDENCE BAG CHALLENGE

You will need: a shoebox, a doll "victim," markers, craft items such as card stock or paper, tape, glue, etc. to decorate your crime scene, a friend

1. Make your own shoebox crime scene. Have a story in mind as you decorate it. Put lots of clues for your friend to use to create a profile about who did it. This "victim" was shot through the window. The clock broke with the blast. The handprint shows the killer only had three fingers and a thumb on their right hand.

2. See if your friend can piece together a profile.

Top Tip

If the killer leaned on the window with his right hand, he probably shot with his left hand.

Covering Their Tracks

Some killers try to cover up their crime by **staging** a crime scene. They may move the body somewhere else to throw detectives off the scent. Often a killer will try to make a death look like an accident, or as if the victim has killed themself.

If someone kills a member of their own household, they might make it look as if the house had been broken into. That throws suspicion away from family members as police look for a burglar instead. Police aren't usually that easily fooled, though. Neither are criminal profilers!

Top Tip

Tobias might be suspicious that this crime scene has been staged. The "burglar" didn't take the jewelry!

Signs of Staging

There are several things that can make police suspicious that a crime scene may not be all it seems.

- There is no sign of a break-in
- The drawers have been dumped out to make the room look obviously ransacked
- The drawers are taken out but neatly stacked
- Some valuables have not been taken
- Only a few particular items have been stolen
- No items have been stolen
- The victim has life insurance
- The victim's death may have helped someone in some way

Solve It!

Which of the things below might make you suspect a crime scene may have been staged?

a) The glass in the kitchen door had been broken. All the broken glass is scattered over the doorstep outside.

b) Bedroom drawers are tipped upside down on the bed. Nothing has been taken.

c) The couple who owned the house had just taken out insurance.

d) All of the above

Answers on page 45

Tracking Down a Killer

Criminal profilers can even give detectives an idea of where a serial killer may live. Geographical profiling, or geoprofiling, is a science where experts map where victims are found and work out where the killer may live from those patterns.

Serial killers usually kill in an area close to where they live. However, they usually avoid killing in what is known as the "buffer zone." The buffer zone is the area very close to their home. They avoid this area as it might mean they are more likely to get caught.

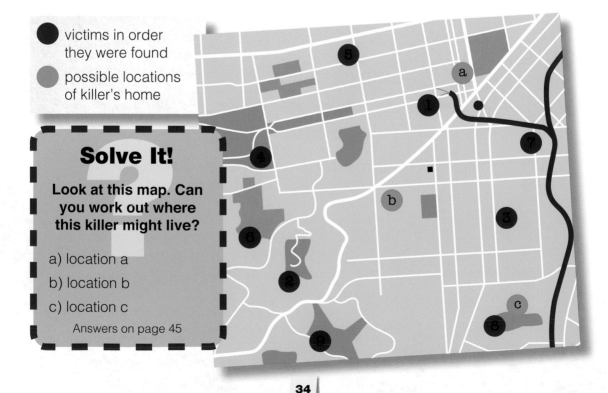

victims in order they were found

possible locations of killer's home

Solve It!

Look at this map. Can you work out where this killer might live?

a) location a

b) location b

c) location c

Answers on page 45

Geoprofiling can predict where a killer may strike next. Those living near recent crime scenes usually become more careful, stay indoors, or avoid lonely spots. This forces the killer to choose another place. If a killer uses public transportation, geoprofilers look at train lines or bus routes to predict where they may go next.

The killer mapped below likes parks near train lines. Where do you think they'll strike next — South Station, Riverside, or Green Park? Answer on page 45.

Answer on page 45.

Top Tip

Experts believe a killer usually lives within a triangle formed by the first three strikes.

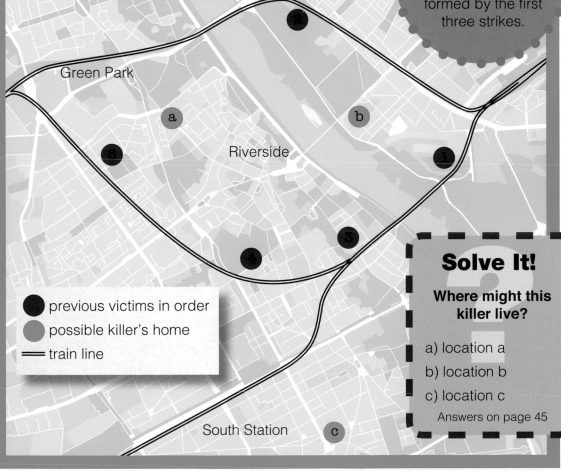

Green Park

a

b

Riverside

previous victims in order
possible killer's home
train line

Solve It!

Where might this killer live?

a) location a

b) location b

c) location c

Answers on page 45

South Station

Detective Smithson shows Tobias a note that has arrived at the police station. He thinks it must be from the killer. Whoever sent the note took care not to write it by hand. Experts can match a person's handwriting if they have enough examples to compare it to.

Dearest Detectives,

So far I have poisoned three people who needed my help. You are being super slow. Catch me quick or I may kill again. More healthy people will get sick quick,

The Hemlock Poisoner

The note didn't give many clues! It was typed and printed on standard paper. Fingerprint experts found nothing. The letter can still help find a suspect, though. People sometimes use unusual signature words when they speak or write. Finding a signature word may help prove the letter was written by a particular person.

Top Tip

The words used can give away information about someone's background. Are they well-educated? Is English their first language?

Searching for Signature Words

Tobias looks back through the interviews of the people working at the health food store. He thinks he finds a signature word match with the note! Can you? Answer on page 45.

Ahmed Ishak
"I always look after my meat until it goes to the store. No one tampers with it until then."

Sarah Crowther
"I just work at the checkout. I handle all the food and medicine, but it is always bagged up."

José Marquez
"I prepare all the drugs except when I have my day off. I never touch the food."

Patricia Nilsson
"As store owner I help out in all departments. That helps us serve customers super quick."

Lie Detectors

The team bring Patricia Nilsson in to ask her a few more questions. Tobias suggests they ask open questions that need more than a "yes" or "no" answer. When Nilsson starts talking she might give herself away.

Police interviewers know how to look for signs that people are lying. Do they look nervous, or blink a lot? Do they look away, or stare? Are they talking too much, or refusing to talk at all? These may be signs that the person is guilty.

Top Tip

Some experts think that if a person is using a lot of hand gestures, they may be lying.

Looking Closely

Looking at **body language** can be the best way to tell whether or not someone is telling a lie. Body language is the combination of a person's gestures, movements, and mannerisms. Ask a friend a question that you know the answer to, such as where they live. Watch their body language. See if their eyes move around, or they fidget in their chair. Now ask your friend to think up a true story about themselves, but also add in one lie. Now that you know how they act when telling the truth, ask them to tell their story. Look out for any change in body language that might show you when they tell you the lie. Did you guess it?

EVIDENCE BAG CHALLENGE

The brain has to work harder when it tells a lie. Put that theory to the test. This experiment sees if telling a lie affects the brain's ability to carry out another task at the same time.

You will need: some friends, a notepad and pen

1. Ask a friend to hold one arm straight out, with their palm facing down. Ask your friend to keep that position while they say some statements. Two of the statements must be true, and one of them will be a lie.

2. Right after your friend says each statement, push down gently on their arm. Use the same amount of force each time you press their arm, so that the experiment is fair.

3. Try the same experiment on some more friends. Write down your results. Was it easier to push their arms after they told the truth, or after they told a lie? What does that tell you?

eparing the evidence

Detectives have enough evidence to accuse Nilsson of the murders. It is time for everyone on the case to get their reports ready. When the case goes to trial they must present the facts correctly. Judges like facts, not opinions.

Criminal profiles are rarely used in court, as they are only a theory and not hard facts. Profiles are used by detectives to help them find the killer. The detectives must then find evidence to support their case.

EVIDENCE BAG CHALLENGE

Judges have to be careful that a **jury** is not influenced by any opinions. It is very easy to be influenced by other people. Try this experiment on some friends.

You will need: a few friends, a ruler, pen and paper

- Draw three lines that are exactly equal in length at different angles on a piece of paper.

- Secretly tell some friends to strongly agree with the line you say is longest.

- Ask the group which line is the longest. Point at the line you have chosen. Your other friends should all agree. Do the ones left out of the secret argue, or agree too? What do your results tell you?

Tobias writes up his report. Occasionally his profile may be used in court as expert evidence. Even though a good deal of criminal profiling is based in science, it is not hard fact. It is up to the detectives such as Doug Smithson to produce the evidence for the lawyers to present in court. Tobias will follow the case with interest. He is always pleased when he knows that his work has helped catch a killer.

Top Tip

Criminal profiling isn't the same as it is shown on TV. A profiler will never crack a case on their own.

The Day Of the Trial

Patricia Nilsson looked like an unlikely serial killer, at first. She was small and slight. She was happily married. She had a successful career, too. In cases of poisoning, though, detectives knew that the killer is often a woman. Size and strength don't matter when it comes to poisoning people.

When Doug Smithson looked into her background, he found that she wasn't as perfect as she first appeared. She had a criminal record for assault. After studying her medical records, he also discovered she had recently been **diagnosed** with an **incurable** illness. Could that be a motive, in some way?

Solve It!

A killer usually has a motive which explains why they do what they do. Why do you think Patricia Nilsson might have become a serial killer?

a) Nilsson had recently found out that she had a deadly illness. This made her jealous of the healthy people that came in to her store. She took her anger out on her customers.

b) Nilsson enjoyed helping out in all departments of the store, but she didn't really know what she was doing. She accidentally mixed the hemlock poison into some of the medicines and food.

Answers on page 45

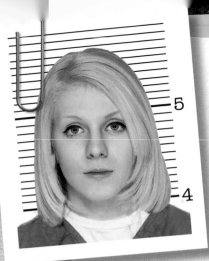

Name: Patricia Nilsson

Date of Trial: 7/22/2018
Court No: Court One
Judge Presiding: T Peabody
Crime: Serial Murder

Profile: Patricia Nilsson had a criminal record. She had once assaulted a woman in a bar. It was discovered that she was the person who called the ambulance for the first two victims!

The lawyers present the evidence. Detectives found hemlock growing at the poultry farm her husband ran. They also found evidence of the poison in the store. They discovered an interesting fact about quail, a bird Nilsson's husband kept at the farm. Quail can happily eat hemlock, but if a person then eats the quail, they'll be poisoned. There is a strong case against Nilsson. Now it's up to the jury to decide. What do you think?

GUILTY or **NOT GUILTY**

Glossary

autopsy An examination of a dead body especially to find out the cause and manner of death.

body language Movements (as with the hands) or posture used as a means of expression.

coincidence Two things that happen at the same time by accident but seem to have some connection.

conclusions Final decisions reached by reasoning.

crime scenes Places where an offense has been committed and forensic evidence may be gathered.

critical thinking The ability to think clearly and rationally about what to do or what to believe.

diagnosed Recognized by signs and symptoms.

DNA The code in each person's cells that makes everyone unique.

evidence Material presented to a court in a crime case.

incurable Not capable of being cured.

inherit To receive by legal right from a person at the person's death.

jury A group of people in court who must decide whether someone is guilty or not.

mental illness Health conditions involving changes in thoughts, emotions, behaviors, or a combination of these.

motive Something that leads or influences a person to do something.

prejudiced Being biased.

profile A report that

shows the important characteristics of something.

reconstruction The act of reconstructing.

serial killer A person who murders three or more people, with the murders taking place over more than a month and including a significant "cooling off period" between them.

staging To produce

something as if on stage.

stereotypes Ideas that many people have about a thing or a group of people and that may often be untrue or only partly true.

suspects Persons thought to be guilty of a crime.

vulnerable Capable of being physically or emotionally wounded.

ANSWERS

page 5 - b, page 9 - ambulance called by passerby, cause of death, page 10 - b, page 11 - 1=c, 2 = e, 3 = f, 4 = a, 5 = d, 6 = b, page 13 - a, 16 - a, page 18 - b, page 21 - 1=b, 2 = f, 3 = a, 4 = e, 5 = d, 6 = c, page 22 - c, page 23 - both a = risk taker, page 25 - c, page 26 - 1 = c, 2 = d, 3 = b, 4 = a, page 29 - d, page 33 - d, page 34 - b, page 35 - Green Park is the next location, the killer lives at - b, 37 - Patricia Nilsson says both "super" and "quick", page 42 - a - the fact she sent a note taunting police means that she intended to kill her victims.

Want to be a Criminal Profiler?

Job: Criminal Profiler

Job Description: Criminal profilers need to be good at critical thinking. They need to be able to find information from many different sources. Then they need to be able to use that information to draw conclusions. Profilers must be used to looking at all the small details, and then piece together a picture.

Qualifications needed: A degree in a science or law subject, then a further master's degree in a science subject such as Psychology. They would usually study human and criminal behavior as part of their master's degree. Many criminal profilers will also have a doctorate in Psychology, too. Profilers will also attend other training courses, such as ones run by the FBI.

Employment: Criminal Profilers work for law enforcement agencies, particularly organizations such as the FBI. Some profilers find work at large companies. Their skills are used to look at people working for the company or applying for jobs there.

Further Information

BOOKS

Beres, D. B. *Killer at Large: Criminal Profilers and the Cases They Solve! (24/7: Science Behind the Scenes: Forensics).* New York, NY: Scholastic, 2007.

Gray, Susan H. *Forensic Psychologist (21st Century Skills Library: Cool STEAM Careers).* North Mankato, MN: Cherry Lake Publishing, 2015.

Websites

Check out the Science Buddies lie detector test project at this cool site!
http://www.sciencebuddies.org/science-fair-projects/project_ideas/HumBio_p019.shtml

Play the PBS Kids Arthur detective game here!
http://pbskids.org/arthur/games/effectivedetective/

PUBLISHER'S NOTE TO EDUCATORS AND PARENTS:

Our editors have carefully reviewed these websites to ensure that they are suitable for students. Many websites change frequently, however, and we cannot guarantee that a site's future contents will continue to meet our high standards of quality and educational value. Be advised that students should be closely supervised whenever they access the Internet.